SILLY RHYMES
AND
THE SUBLIME

Insights On Life's
Peaks And Valleys

DOLORES ROLLINS

TO MY DEAR FRIENDS OF WRITER'S INK

CONTENTS

1JOYS

A Dozen Survival Techniques

Here's what to do to survive;

1) Be silly or die.

2) Belly laugh with the brood;
   Do not do this with a mouthful of food.

3) Cuddle a baby;
   Be careful if wet and smelly.

4) A dog or a cat you can pat;
   But not a rat.

5) Have a relaxing, delicious meal;
   Not served on the back of a seal.

6) Eat your vegetables!
   "Says Dr. Dolly":
   They are delectable and palatable".

7) Sleep well, pleasant dreams!
   In the dark, don't let in creepy, crawly things,
   Only angels with gossamer wings.

8) Slouch on the couch.
   Burp and scratch and yawn.
   Watch T.V. until dawn.

9) Sing, dance, play sports.
   Happily shout from the rooftops;
   Until someone tells you to stop.

10) Run in the fields, stop to smell flowers.
    This is best done in daylight hours.

11) Have lunch with a friend,
    As if the day will never end.

12) Observe life passing by
    Without a critical eye.
    If you do all this,
    You will get bliss;
    But I don't guarantee.
    Don't expect your money back from me.

    *Bonus Special note.
    Tickling is also a survival technique.
    Try it you might like it; it's the most unique.

    My Pastime Stew

    *Singing and cooking as if I am Anthony Bourdain,
    This is my refrain:
    "I never use a cookbook;
    But, sometimes it pays to take a look".

    *When I travel to a foreign land, my mind to expand;
    Careful!, it can also enlarge your waistband.
    Especially, when tasty delicacies are piled high;
    On huge plates that would make an elephant cry.

    Additionally, I offer impractical advice
    For the wise:
    *When you eat pakora;
    Do not wear your fedora,
    It's not kosher.

    After all that,
    *Exercise is good to lose fat.
    It does not count when only lips flap.

    *As of late,
    I meditate,
    Cogitate,
    Gravitate towards:
    Books in bed or in the shed or in the head.
    It is said,
    Reading makes you smart.;

Even if it comes from Walmart.

And......
*Ancient history,
To me is a mystery.
It could reveal something of the self.
Maybe, once I was a little elf.

And......
*I swim with all my crooked limbs.
I do the crawl
To the edge of a waterfall
And never fall over the rim.

*I share a funny fact:
Knitting is made of wooly string,
Woven in textural knots,
Bought in colorful lots.
At the end, beware, get enough
Because finding matching colors is tough.

*"Playing piano is, sometimes, such fun.
Lessons of which I have had none.
Even though chords and keys
Are a mystery.
I still play on,
For I have a song
In my heart that needs to be sung".

That makes nine.
For me, the above are all very fine.

Serendipity

I went to visit the bayou,
One beautiful, sunny day
To play with my bright, quick friend;
Who could be right around the bend.
My heart leaps.
He is there,
Gracefully sliding in and out, fin in the air.

I am far away from my friend.
I have to run around the bend.
People are watching his antics.
I am nearly frantic;
That he'll go away
And I'll not see him today;
But I send a thought.
It's not all for naught.
I arrive.
He dives
He slips in and out of water at a frantic pace.
I run with great glee.
It's a great race;
Back and forth,
We are side by side.
I run breathlessly beside
The wall to watch him
Swim .
As this incredible wild animal
Spins away.
Sadly, no more play, today.

2 HUMANS

The Human Machine

The human machine starts out as a cute ball of hairless, bawling flesh. The machine does not come with instructions on how to operate it. Somehow, we learn to use it, after many failed attempts. The bumbling, small mass grows into a great piece of workmanship. That is youth, the ultimate beauty and power. Maturity retains its good looks; but glasses signal things to come.

Menopause messes with the woman's thermostat. When the 60's arrive, the mechanism starts changing rapidly. As the years pass, your hair starts to manufacture white strands, which spread in the intervening years. Other hairy sprouts pop up in the oddest places, like a woman's face or a man's nose or ears (strange that the top of the head on men becomes shiny and bald, (given that it has migrated to other places). Snippers take care of women's facial hair. Good luck to the men.

The suit of skin begins to sag, with no hope of relief from all the wrinkle creams in the world. It looks like wearing a cotton garment to bed. The gears need some grease at this point, but will it help? Rest for the machine gets interrupted by draining the plumbing. Picking up sounds becomes spotty. Then, the brain begins to fudge up. For example: forgetting why you went into a room for some important mission. Or, losing things, when you know they are here somewhere, just temporarily misplaced. They can't be lost. Ha!

Time flies at light speed. Are we slowing down?

It's a short life and one must make the most of it; even though the parts are gumming up. I feel I have opened up as a person; despite society's prejudice about the worth of old people. After all, we don't lose all our powers all at once. I am not ready for the junkyard, yet.

You have to live until the engine dies; and maybe even that is not the end. We may come back with another newer machine or continue elsewhere with a shiny, new flying saucer.

Sounds great doesn't it, or does it? I'll let you decide.

Men

Not all men are good.
Not all men are bad.
Below describe the lads:
Men are fun;
But they keep you on the run.
Men like meat.
They say it is good to eat.
They also say "relax,
Let the cleaning go lax.
I know how to do things.
After all, I am a man.
I can:
Build a house.
Catch a mouse.
Fix a truck,
With any luck.
I work well with wood,
See aren't my toys good?
Diapers I do not do.
That is up to you".
These are the men I have known.
They have to be shown.
That they are not always right.
I tell them every night.
Oh my, do they get uptight
About various things
Like women's zings
Don't they know that women are perfect?
Do I hear a resounding no?
What the heck?
That cannot be so.

3 LOVE

My Son

You were a wonder as a first child.
Watching that little blond head
Pop out of bed.
I was glad,
You had
A special bond with my Dad.
He was a good man,
like you.
When did I grow older?
When did you?
When times are hard,
"Says this bard",
Keep your sense of humor
(at your core).
Above all, I wish I could see you more.

My Cute Little Girl

My cute little girl
Was always in a whirl.
She is going to be a mother
Of Another
New life.
Who will it be?
A her or a him
That will join her in the gym/or swim,

Or stay with Dad in front of the screen,
Or something in between.
This is exciting!

Piper's Lullaby

Sleep is creeping up on baby.
 Let yourself be swept away.
 Where you can dream of wondrous things; you to us will bring.
And when you wake; we will be there.
 So, have no fear.
 When you're feeling blue, you can come to me.
The blues will go-o, you wait and see-e.

Piper's Story

Piper was flying around the vast cosmos, when she received an urgent message from her mother-to-be. She answered the call. The conversation went like this; (Tina)-"I need you to be with me soon". (Piper)-"OK Mom, I am ready. How will I find you?" (Tina)-"Just let the light of love guide you".

So, the little darling dropped down to earth. She landed hard. Her first day on this planet looked like her last. But, she chose, to the delight of her two parents and me, to go home with them. She made us all happy. She spent the first two weeks dozing. She still had one foot in this world and one foot in another. To make up for lost time, she drank deep from nature's well. She gained much strength in the lap of her mother's love.

Her smile is as bright as the midday sun. She has love written all over her face. She is now quite strong; despite the rough start. She demonstrates her power, daily, with baby jumping jacks. She is a gift straight from the stars. In this dark world, she'll sparkle like sunset sparks on rippling water.

Right now, she's Mom's little buttercup and Memere's belle petite fille (lovely granddaughter).

I wish her well on her life's journey; for it's a bumpy road.

A Bird's Tale

A long time ago, I used to watch the slim, white herons at the nearby, small, crystalline lake with a fountain. I am a small, white dove. I am alone, since my mate died. I envy their close relationships.

One fine day, as I arrive to enjoy the scenery at this lovely lake, I notice a lone heron. He is not with the others, because there is something wrong with his leg. I approach him cautiously; because he is a lot bigger bird. I ask him what is wrong. He is very thin and alone. He says: "When I was young, I fledged too early and hit the ground hard and hurt my leg". He is now a lot older and the leg injury keeps resurfacing. This time he could not walk, nor scrounge for food. He is alone like me. He asked a few other herons if they could help, but they were too busy. Strangely enough, I hurt my wing recently by crashing into a closed window. I had eaten too many fermented berries.
I was not as badly injured as he. So, I could help him scavenge for food. I helped him until he could walk again, on his own. We do not eat the same things; but it works, nevertheless.

We somehow managed to heal simultaneously. From then on, we meet on a regular basis to hunt or fish. Now that we are feeling better, on weekends, we fly to the beach to observe the humans.

What an unlikely pair we are; but we have become friends.

Where Is Love?

Birds fly.
People die.
But where is love hiding?
Is it locked in a drawer, to be taken out only on special occasions?
Is it hiding under the couch in the dark, shying away, waiting to come out?
Is it stuck in the closet, waiting to be let out?
Is it hiding in the bushes, until the cacophony ends?
Is it a night-blooming flower waiting to unfold in the moon glow?
Is it lurking in the shadows, waiting for the dawn to break?
Is it in the bottomless pit; but sees the pinhole of light from above?
Does love survive the worst calamities?
Is love alive?

It is alive in the racing heartbeat at the sight of the lover.
It is in the wag of a dog's tail when it sees its master.
It is behind the front door of the home, safe and warm.
It is in the eye of the new mother for her newborn,
And in the newborn for her.
It is in the heart of the grandmother,
Watching the child grow and develop.
It is in the smile of a Down's Syndrome child.
Love is in the small things we do for others.
Is love alive?

It is. It is.

Flowers

Flowers grow
If they know,
They are a part
Of your heart.

They share their graces
In beautiful vases.
For you, they glow.

Flowers don't grow
For a hardened heart.
They break apart,
They cry,
They die.

Dream Time

I am in an odd dream. I am in Mexico with a male companion. He sees beauty everywhere and I see it too; but I also see the ugliness. It is a weird mix of people around me who are very friendly. They laugh a lot Their families are very strong. The get together all the time. Mainly, because they live close to each other. They share everything they have, even their lives. They know all about each individual family member. Their gorgeous women have large families. Lots of their children have birth defects. I do not understand the reasons why.

I go to strange places with him, full of unfamiliar smells, tastes, and sights. There is overwhelming poverty. For example: hot water is available only some of the time.   A single bathroom is for four people. Many families only have a curtain for a door. Folks sell dead chickens on the street, and eggs from the birds are sitting nearby in the hot sun. Flies are everywhere. Dry dust gets kicked up from the parched land. The roads in the smaller towns are made of different sizes of uncut rocks. The people seem to survive, despite all this.

They are creative in their endeavors. Businesses sprout up from backs of cars or a blanket spread out on the sidewalk. There is danger involved, such as: people who bob in and out of traffic at red lights; either selling things or cleaning windshields for a living, until the light turns green. God help them survive. The store fronts have large speakers that blare loud music into your ears, to get your attention.

Other weird businesses are: crammed buses that take a route that is not a road, by a lake, without drowning the customers. Images of Frida Kahlo dance around in my head.

The man I am with loves it all. He is intensely passionate about his family and Mexico. We are an odd couple from different cultures.

This dream is so strange, I can hardly believe it. Somebody wake me up.

Maybe life is nothing but a dream.

The Delicate Flower

In the dense forest, there lives a small, delicate, fragrant flower surrounded by huge boisterous blooms, whose roots are spreading out and are crowding the little one. This patch does not allow the little flower to spread her fragrance. She is different from the giants that let her know at every opportunity. She feels like a weirdo. She, also, feels inferior to the big blossoms.

She need some support before she stops unfolding, or sinks into the earth, depressed and alone. There was another like her; but it withered and died. She often wonders if there are others like her, somewhere.

The big ones think she stinks. She agrees she may be stinking or maybe not. She I confused. All she knows is that she is different from the rest.

Will she give up or try to bloom and spread her scent anyway, in this harsh environment?

Flowers of a Kind-Chapter 1

I am a small flower, whose fragrance spreads throughout my world. From my perch by the window, I glow in the low light. Someone cares for me. I feel protected. I watch from my quiet seat, all that goes on. I had a companion; but it died. I hear whispers from afar, that it will be replaced.

But, for now, from my solitary view, I watch the wildflowers outside, who seem to bask in the sun, wind, and harsh storms. I need the quiet inner world that I cannot get out there. I admire them. They seem so strong. I feel weak compared to them. But, their life is not what makes me grow. I close up outside.

At times, I gingerly step outside, to be with the wildflowers and their noisy fun. But, I tire of them and they think I stink.

So, after a while, let me go back inside my bower, to bask in the quiet glow.

Flowers of a Kind-Chapter 2

I am a small, fragrant flower, quietly sitting on my perch by the window. I am happy; but lonely. They care for me. Someone whispered about replacing my dead companion. I watch as the caregivers bring in another plant and set it down beside me. It is a big, strong, cactus. They set him too close to me. His spines are a source of tension. Can I handle this?

My world has changed dramatically. My quiet solitude is interrupted by the burly interloper. He requires more care than I do. So, my needs are not completely satisfied. He is growing fast. Will there be room for me on the perch?

I felt solitary. I wanted a companion. My companion's needs are always greater than my own. So, what to do ?

Go outside with the noisy wildflowers ? No

Maybe he is on loan ?

Maybe I am asking for too much. I am not a perfect plant. Some people think I stink. Even though, I consider myself fragrant. After all, the cactus is a good companion. But oh, beware of the spines.

When he tries to take root in my pot, I have to stand my ground and tell him he cannot take over the territory.

What a life !!

Flowers of a Kind-Chapter 3

The big cactus is still growing, developing, fast. I am the little, fragrant flower next to him on the shelf by the sunny window. He is casting his shadow so that my sunlight is blocked. I need sun to keep me radiant and send out my perfume He still has large needs, that are greater than my own. I have felt his spines pricking into me.

Even so, he does have ingratiating qualities. He shares the tasty plant food from the caregivers. He doesn't drop his dead spines and cactus pads in my small pot.

Maybe we can co-exist peacefully?

Where are the providers? I need to talk to them.

Flowers of a Kind-Chapter 4

This fragrant little flower talked to the providers, about her problems with the Mexican cactus.

This is what they said: "You were here first. What is your heart's desire?"

The wilting blossom said: " He is cutting out my sunlight most of the time. He is pricking me some of the time. I will not bloom well with him obstructing my view. So he has got to go."

They replied: "Your wish be done. We will move him to a drier environment. He will be placed in a different room. "

"Now, I am alone, not totally content; but I can bloom and spread my perfume more easily; because I have freedom to be and to bask in the sunlight that is so crucial to my existence."

The providers care.

Flowers of a Kind-Chapter 5

This lovely violet-blue flower regrets asking the providers to move the huge, Mexican cactus. My only reservation is the lack of companionship, on my perch, by the sun splashed window. At least, the space has expanded.

I asked to have him removed because his stinging spines were growing into my tender flesh. He grew so fast, he created an eclipse of my sun. His roots were spreading all over my quiet perch. He required much of the provider's attention.

16

I missed being placed outside to watch the pretty, lively wildflowers.

I am enjoying my forays into their boisterous world; more than before. The cactus is happier in his own realm, away from my scent. He thought I stunk. He can grow better in the roomier, drier garden; where he flourishes when his blossoms mature into succulent fruit.

Flowers of a Kind-Chapter 6

This is an update from the blue-violet lavender plant.
The providers have place me outside to get some fresh air and sunshine. This is good for me on two levels. I get out to watch others and I get a change of scenery. The scenery is very inspiring.
Their fun is not my kind of fun.

The day is bright, crisp with a strong, refreshing breeze. The sky is clear. All is well. Suddenly, I spot an eagle riding the wind currents. He is coming my way. The closer he gets, I notice a white object in his beak. It is a piece of paper that he drops. It hits me on one of my blossoms and it drops to the ground. This is a surprise; because I don't often see things drop out of the sky, especially when it is delivered by such a big, beautiful bird.

The wildflowers laugh loudly. They think it is funny that it hit me. One wildflower offers to read it to me.

I am appalled. It is from the Mexican cactus. It is a warning. He says if he ever sees me again, he will definitely stick one of his spines deeply into my flesh. He is very upset that I asked the providers to move him away from me. He was happy when he was in control of my small perch. I was not. When his roots began to overrun the tiny perch and his spines got too close, he scared me.

Despite all of that, I still say: "God bless him and God bless me."

In a few days, the eagle returned and dropped another message for me that says: "I love you" from the same source.

????????????????

The wildflower titters.

Dear Jim

Have not heard from you in a while.
It's not your style.
How could this happen?
It's not in the pattern.
So, I wrote you a letter,
To make my self feel better.
"So many things you've missed.
So, here's the list:
From Maine I was sent,
A boyfriend came and went,
Petunia's pregnancy
With a (twin) baby.
Having a hard time
Trying to summer in Maine.
Let me know how
It is in heaven,
Where you play and strum.
So, when I come,
I can join in."

Ma

When I was young
I thought you were no fun.
I felt I could not be myself,
The little elf

Maybe it was not you;
Because now, I see what's true.
I am a lot like you.
You are caring and smart.
You have a big, generous heart.
Independent, you are,
That will take you far.
Family is important there is no doubt.
You taught me what it is all about.
Not too much more to say, except;
You are my mother.
There is not another.
Let's keep special, our times together;
So that we will remember
Forever What we had,
And be glad.

Friendship

Friendships grow,
Friendships thrive;
At times for a long while.
The difficult day is the one
When you have to leave.
It is as if they die away.
It is a time to mourn,
A time to yearn for others
To fill in the heart holes.
No one can be replaced,
Each is a gem of its own.
So, as I roam,
I moan; but
Look for other jewels
To bring me joy.

Year's End

Year's end finds me looking into the rear view mirror of past events.
The highlights, I will try to condense.

First, my new compact hideaway gives glimpses of patchwork pines, tulip
trees, palm trees that sway.

Then, spending time with my family that cares enough to have me.

And a quiet friend who loves beach walks; where birds show us how to
whirl and glide in the sky. Some scurry on thin legs on fine sand.
When the goddess of the sea cleans house and tosses dead mollusks our
way, her gifts we gather. We top if off with a refreshing swim in emerald
waters. The farm is our next destination, to gather the fruits of the farmer's
labor. The green goodies from the gods, make the tummy feel warm. The
jewels of the sea will adorn a box for holding earthly treasures. Some of the
discarded homes of the sea creatures are decorated with stripes and
crisscrossing lines. Others are shaped like pointy whirls or are pearlescent
inside or like turbans or paw shapes. There are interiors of purple, others
translucent in shades of yellow or orange or winged shapes of orange,
purple and pink.

In this mirror I also see, days alone with the grand-baby, strolling around
the tiny lake; peeping at birds who are looking for a breakfast snack. The
crocks wait for a mistake. The cast of characters include: a couple of
roseate spoonbills, all kinds of herons, ducks, and squirrels. Of special
interest to me is the spoonbill, a splashy creature with pink eyes, an orange
muddy spatulate bill, red legs and underbelly, pink wings with wingtips
dripping red. Half submerged in the mud, his head sways from left to right.
What will he/she find?

The mirror does not reveal any unpleasantness. I feel blessed observing
unique Florida life; but my time here is quickly winding down.

I will miss friends I've made here and all the activities I participate in; but, I
need some place cooler with quieter walks in the woods.

A new life awaits.

4 BABIES

Me

I run here there and everywhere.
I am in constant motion with no particular destination.
My steps are a little wobbly.
Gravity is not my friend.
Things get boring easily.
Concentration is tough for me.
Despite all that , I still test my limits regularly.
Fitting my body in tight places is a challenge I love.
I can do anything except put things back together
When I take them apart.
Handling oversize objects is easy most of the time,
When they do not drag me down.
It is important to put objects in their places.
Even when others think they are in odd places.
I have my own sense of order.
Eating with gusto is a joy;
Even though my clothes get covered with food.
I dare you to get me to change.
Bathing is a sometime thing.
Touching all I see is a great pastime (that includes women).
Am I a toddler or a drunk?

A Day With the Grand-Baby

"Baby, baby,
You make me crazy.
First, it was the dirt
You played in and
Wanted to touch me.
Then it was your runny nose

That got all over me.
Then it was your dirty didee.
I have to be careful not to get any on me.
You say you want to play in the toilet.
Oh, no, no, no!
Or you want to inspect the diaper pail.
No, no, no!
Or dig up your mother's plants.
No, no, no!
Or throw your toys.
No, no, no!
Or go into the garbage.
No, no, no!
As you spin around to get dizzy,
Or dribble your bottle of milk on the floor.
Or when you open and empty cabinets and empty drawers.
I've had enough of your mischief.
What do I say when you come to me, all gooey.
Do I say no, no, no?
I say yes, yes, yes.
Come to me lovely little child."

Eighteen Months

Watching her makes my head spin.
She comes in, she goes out.
Spreads her things all about.
She crawls into cabinets,
She takes pans out.
Squawks come from her when things get tough.
Then is when I've had enough.
Throws her lunch down,
While dogs all hang around
Waiting for a snack.
"Here's one for you Zak".
Run around with no destination.
What in tarnation?
That's the aim of the game

With no name.
This leads to frustration
From the previous generation.
I wait for a nap break.
This child does not nap;
For her it is just a bunch of crap.
I won't mention her nappies.
I gather my gloves, wipes, diaper and blankie.
Try not to get any on me.
It's a trick
Being a hands-on grannie.
This will definitely
Get you off your fanny.

Split Personality

I am two halves.
One is loud, proud
Waiting to be heard,
With repercussions and
No discussions.
My frustrations
Create aggravations
All around.
I will be heard!
Or I am going to trash everything you own.

From my other side,
I have a different point of view.
All smiles, I am enthusiastic.
How ironic
Can this be?
I am so pretty.
I run to and fro,
Eager to know
All that needs to be discovered
In the cupboards,
Nooks and crannies,
I go.
Danger is a constant presence.

The essence of which,
I do not care to know.
I am this dichotomy.
Please do not suggest a lobotomy!

5 DREAMS

What If

What if there was no starvation,
No greed,
No anger,
No intolerance,
No laziness,
No lying,
No arguments,
No pretension,
No domination,
No cruelty,
No cheating,
No sarcasm,
No torture,
No nationalism,
No religious fanaticism,
In the world; only co-operation, justice, peace and all people living up to
their full potential.

What kind of a world would it be?
Dream along with me.

6 SPIRITUALITY

Coat of Many Colors

At home, I am a being bathed in delight.
Born naked,
I am wrapped in rags.
I yearn for more.
Then wrapped in white linen.
I find myself upward bound.
Then wrapped in wool,
I sense not the cold.
Then wrapped in silk,
A lightness of soul.
Wrapped in silver,
I shimmer in the light of the moon.
Wrapped in gold,
I sparkle in the midday sun.
Wrapped in white light,
Where all is bright,
There it ceases to be dark.
I am going home!

Plain Talk To God

God, if you are there,
Hear my prayer.
Why did you make me forget what I came here to do?
You left me with no clue.
Half of the time, I don't know where I am going,

Or what I am doing.
At this great age, I thought I would be unbelievably wise;
But, big surprise!
I know nothing more
Than before.
Well, maybe a little more.
Some want to grab the greatest power and money they can.
But, I do not follow this plan.
Where all around me is madness.
Give me strength for gladness.
People can be quite funny in their lunacy;
If you look at it honestly.
I still hold to be true,
What I feel I must do;
Even though others may think I am crazy
Or maybe lazy.
Of that I am weary.
I think God's response to me would be:
"Never fear, live love, laugh and be happy!"

Who Are We? Where Did We Come From, Where Are We Going?

It's interesting how we forget from where we came.
Is it all a game?
A meaningless game?
We need to heed the signs
That come sometimes,
To help us along,
To remember where we belong.
Most of the time, we come and go,
To and fro,
Without knowing
Exactly what to do,
Lost in the stew.
Take some time,
Some quiet time
To reflect on why we are here
It's not so queer an idea.

Try it!
You may find something wonderful there.

7 PROBLEMS

Medical Woes Chapter 1

Hold your breath and pinch your nose.
So, here goes.
Went to the Minute Clinic,
Very scientific; but no picnic.
"Fill out a computer form".
Is this the new norm?
You have to learn
To sit and wait your turn.
The doors open,
It's your time to whine.
"Welcome to my medical closet".
Said the young nurselet.
"First show me your papers.
Swollen finger, ding dong!
Got a recipe for you.
First, I must offer you
A shot for flu;
Then prescribe some medical goo.
OK, all done.
What's the sum?
Will send you a bill.
Just put me in your will.
Next!"

Medical Woes Chapter 2

The meds the little nurse gave me
1,2,3
Made me ill.
No more green pills.
For this old woman

Is goin'

Medical Woes Chapter 3

To another clinic with doctors who cut;
But,
For now fill out a form.
Then again wait your turn.
"The doctor will see you in time.
Just don't whine".
Here he comes with needle and knife.
He created a lot of strife;
But cut out the pus.
"Here's where I cuss.
That hurt!"

Medical Woes Chapter 4

"With the meds, the finger is healing
But, I am not feeling
Great.
This I hate.
Maybe tomorrow, I will get a break!"

Women's Problem

When I was young and all parts of my "corps" worked well. I thought, it will be great to retire. After all the work of redoing houses, raising kids and working are over. We will just have fun. You know: travel.

No one mentions that as you get older and have less responsibilities, some changes occur in the "corps". Some changes that were not to my liking. As grey hair started sprouting in my dark hair, I silently yelled "Eek!" After menopause, the changes started accelerating. Menopause hit me like the sky fell on me. I had terrible sweats. So much, so that I would have to strip down to bare essentials when entering a warm, winter house. I remember putting my head in the freezer, in those first few summers. Sleeping was not as easy as it had been. I had to wait until the last flash burned me up, before closing my eyes. I would throw off all the covers to cool the fires, again. God forbid, if I woke up in the night; then the flashes ignited again. When I taught, I always prayed that the flash would cool down; by the time I turned to the class from the blackboard. My face would light up like a red light bulb, announcing to the world what was happening internally. It was very embarrassing.

After all that, I vowed to go to a hot flash workshop; put on by a competent medical person. The nurse reported that flashes are confined to head, neck and upper chest. When I feel my feet burning up in my shoes, I think of her. I was doubtful about her medical knowledge. She also claimed, ten to twelve years of flashes, was all one would have to endure. I am at year eighteen, and still own them. Chocolate and brown drinks were to be avoided; she said. I am willing to pay the price for chocolate.

So, I had a choice; either take estrogen or try herbal remedies. So, I am not waiting for the flashes to stop; to do all things I ever wanted to do. I just keep on trucking with cool thoughts and drops of sweat trailing behind me.

Dr. Li

Here she comes.
"Take off your clothes.

I do not want you to doze.
Lie down,
Don't frown.
I need to insert
A small needle to see if it hurts."
Cat's claws sink in to my tender flesh.
A voodoo doll comes to mind.
She may give the pins a twist
To see if I resist.
Then tells me to lift
My bad arm as far as I can.
I can only reply "yes ma'am."
Other tricks she picks:
Are glass cups that suck,
Just a little blood
To clear out the crud.
"First, I light it up
With a big flame.
Sorry, close to your face I came?
You'll look like a big octopus
Grabbed you to eat.
What a treat !"
Now that I am all tied up,
A small, Chinese bridge
On me, pumps out herbal smoke;
That's no joke!
"Now that you're are done on one side,
Flip over
For more fun."

I know she is not mean.
She is the queen,
Who does it all with a smile.
So, that all that torture
Is worthwhile.

Life's Little Difficulties

At times I understand a lot;
Often I know naught.
When tragedy strikes,
I feel alive with bad vibes.
God calm me down,
So I have no frown.
My life is all askew.
When Is it going to renew?
House is going,
Surgery is coming.
God where are you when I need you?
Maybe when this is all through,
I will be good as new?

Life's Ups and Downs

Life dishes out dirty dishwater
Now and again.
One more misery pops up,
Like mushrooms sprout up,
Out of nowhere.
Let's meditate and sit back
And cool off, think twice!
Be nice!
Don't blow your stack,
Stay on track.
This will pass.
It always does;
Like all the others did
Without life ending.
I challenge you
To try
This new way!
Pull out of the fray!

It's gonna' continue anyway.

2017

Humans are on the brink,
I think,
Of devastating wars.
What are we the powerless to do?
Let the powerful grab what they can?
They do not plan for the consequences of
Their power grabs.
After their Big Bang,
The earth will recover;
But without us, humans.
Unless there is a solution
To that thirst for power.
Equality is its name.

Screw Inspection Chapter 1

One fine day, I decided to replace my original 1950's windows in the Florida room. I called a window and door company to make an appointment. They showed up one bright, early, lovely morning. They worked very fast. They pulled out the ancient ones. I was nosily listening to all the noises they were making as they were releasing the old window, (if you want to call them that). There were not many working parts on these old things. I could hear things like: "I can't believe this or @##XXX!!!." This made me shiver. I hoped things were going OK ???????? When they walked through with one set of battered windows; I was not sorry to see them go. I looked to see how things were going. I saw my apartment now had an incredible, open air view to the sun, grass and tree-lined back lawn.

A short time later, they quickly put in place the brand-new windows; framed with plastic and put up with shiny new screws. They were in an incredible hurry. As the workman was leaving, he demonstrated how to open the windows. They are heavy. I started to pull off the stickers that were on the windows. He informed me that I should not do that until the screw inspection was over. Screw inspection????? Never heard of that one up North. I was to call for an appointment for the screw inspector????????
As the workman picked up his tools. He said he would return for the rest. I sneaked a look at the windows. I noted that the caulking was sloppy(I worked on our new house with Jim's instructions). I complained to him. He came back with a wet rag to straighten out the lines. I looked again; they were pretty much the same. He said I should paint over the edge of the caulking. What?????? "Don't you have any paint in that closet?" No, I did not. I can't match the paint I used. It was custom mixed. As all paints are today.

I know when to quit, (no sense in arguing with the worker). I was not happy. I called the company. They said the manager would call for an appointment to look at the messy caulking. Now, I need a caulk inspection. I haven't seen or heard from them yet. I have learned a lesson. I was planning to use them next year to do the front windows. No way, will I use them again!!!!!!

The state certified screw inspector showed up in a timely manner and approved of the screw job. I asked his opinion on the caulking job. He said it looked like they were working fast. Ha!

How many more inspections do I need? Have you ever had a state certified screw inspector visit you?

Anyone can have the name of this company. Ask me later.

As a postscript, my daughter and son-in-law got a huge tickle out of the story about the screws. My son-in-law has a great sense of humor. You can imagine in what direction his thoughts were moving.

Screw Inspection Chapter 2

My front windows were replaced in 2 hours, one fine day.
No big deal, wouldn't you say?
I am waiting for the county screw inspector;
(the protector).
Have to hang around until he decides,
It is time to arrive.
I get really restless;
Waiting for the stress
Of his critical gaze
To tell me everything is OK?
(uh oh! I see the screens are on backwards)
He comes after I wait and I wait;
Only to tell me the screws are not tight.
So we have to start all over again,
With another inspection
To see if we pass.
I'm feeling I'm in a morass,
Or a hamster in a cage.
No sense in getting into a rage.
Somehow this waste of time,
Must have a purpose.
Or is it just a circus?
I've got to believe there is some sense
To this nonsense.
Maybe not?

Screw Inspection Chapter 3

There was a knock at the door. It was a giant of a man, with a humble demeanor, politely asking to come in. He was a gentle giant. This tall man represented Pinellas County (the screw inspector).

He came early this time. I did not have to wait around all day long. He inspected the pile of paperwork from the window company. He mumbled

to himself. He then went to the big bay window, carefully inspecting every part. The giant slid open the window and gently closed it. He came towards me and asked to see the rear windows. I told him: "No, no they were done one year ago; but you could look at the small front bedroom window. It was done at the same time as the big one you just looked at. "
He quietly shuffled off to the front. I went back to what I was doing. I heard him playing with the windows. In a short while, he popped his head out of the small room. He came forward, with a smile on his face. He reservedly said, "yeah,! you passed this time". All is well. I joined him with an enthusiastic "yeah" of my own. Thank God! This situation has dragged on for weeks. I am free at last. Or so I thought.

In summary, here's how the crazy story went with the company. They came one day and left in one day. The joint compound was put on in a sloppy manner. I stopped the chief at the end of the two hour job and asked for the joints to be cleaned up. He did a good job. I have done work on my own house and know what quality work looks like.

I later discovered the screens were on backwards. So I called for another visit. I could have done the work but was not willing to do that, after having paid them in full.

The first inspection failed due to the window company submitting the wrong paperwork. The second inspection passed. Then I got a call from the company asking for another appointment to install the plastic covers for the screws. I said "no thanks, I can do it by myself". I refuse to stay at home waiting for these guys. I suddenly remember, after putting the phone down, that I do not recall a plastic cover for the small bedroom window. I called them again, to ask for the second plastic screw cover. They responded by wanting to make another appointment. I couldn't sit and spin my wheels again, waiting for the workers to show up. They agreed to it by leaving it outside.

I hope this is the end of the tale.

?????????????????????????????????????

Stand by for the boring sequel.

The Good Old Days

Remember when you went to the movies for twenty-five cents? My parents thought that was expensive.

Why, I remember doctors actually coming to your home. They charged practically nothing. Now you can become bankrupt with one hospital stay. Or a loss of a tooth, may result in busting your budget.

Or, remember when service in any business was really backed up with superior service and not delays in servicing or excuses for no service at all; followed by months of complaining to contentious, adamant customer service reps.

The snail mail I receive is tremendous. I just throw it away.

Or, when you called someone, they either answered or they were not at home. No playing phone tag several frustrating times.

Or, when there was no e-mail to check or phone messages or facebook pages. Internet is crucial today. How did we survive without it. Innumerable passwords are spilling over in my head. Today, identity theft is common. When I was ten, we bought a TV (with no color, of course). I could actually turn a knob and have it come on right away. Today I have to turn power on and wait for it to cycle itself. You had tapes of music that you could actually rewind to the spot that you liked.

Appliances used to last forever. No short term warranties were issued back then.

Cars could last more than 5 years, if well cared for. They could be cared for in those day, by most men. Now you need a computer to tell you what's wrong. What happens if you lose power on the day that your car is in the garage being fixed. I just love cranking down window in cars. But, you cannot do that today, if you turn the key off. Strange that there are no wipers in the rear of some cars and the headlights are constantly on.

Even the grocery stores or banks are crippled when their computers are down. The unbelievable part is everyone relies on the computer to tell them how much change to give the customer. Whatever happened to thinking for yourself.

I guess I must be a leftover from the stone age. I want to bake bread, can stuff, knit, draw. All these things do not require training on a computer.

Yin, Yang

Can't make up my mind,
To stay or go.
Love or hate,
Runaway or wait.
Lie down or run.
Which would be the most fun?
Drive or ride a bike or walk,
Say something or not talk.
To eat to fill and feel ill.
To eat or dine
Maybe with wine?
To cook in the microwave,
Or make food from scratch, be brave!
So many things to do.
Do many or just a few?
Always think about gain
Or to refrain.
To marry or tarry,
Meditate or vegetate.
Keep old friends or make new,
Which?
Oh, hell let's just have some fun.

State of Maine Blues

Married a Mainer true and true, had a time getting it out of you.
Poor old Maine, I hate to complain.
But most of the time, your weather's insane,
I have the State of Maine, lack of sunshine blues.

Maine is home but don't get me wrong.
I don't care much for a winter's storm.
When that happens, I seek a sunny clime.
I need that warm Fla. sunshine.
Don't get me wrong, Maine summer is nice.
I have the State of Maine winter, snowbird blues.

State of Maine, State of Maine, to where my ancestors came.
I got the cold, dark, loony state of Maine blues.

Maine in summer, has lots but beware.
Spring in Maine , nothing but rain;
Summer's nice to drive away those Me. snowbird blues.
Fireside chats are not for me.
I got the cold, snowy, no sun, state of Maine blues.

Florida

Florida, Florida, how I loved you.
Even wrote a song about you.
Like any new love,
When the flame goes out;
The ashes reveal a heat.
The heat you impart
Is more than my heart

Can bear.
Noise from the traffic
Is more than I care
To hear.
Too may people out and about,
In the streets causes:
Beeping and screeching of brakes.
I yearn for quieter climes,
Cooler sunrises, and
Times more sublime.

Virginia

One day while meandering in the forest, I met a woman named Virginia. She was walking my way as the first rays of the sun were streaking from the horizon. She came towards me with arms wide open, waiting to embrace me as the gentle breeze blew through her long, golden hair. She wore a long, white, silk gown. She led me through a field of wildflowers with a strong scent of wild roses. She brings good fortune. She is accompanied by many lively spirits. She wishes me well as she turns towards the sunset.

As the shadows lengthen, I see someone coming out of the shadows. Her name is also Virginia; but dark shadows encircle her. Her hair hangs in dark, greasy, matted, stringy strands. Her dress is ragged and blackened by smoke. She wants me to stumble into her dark, snake-infested cave. She says she can give me a boon; if I step inside the dark lair. She pulls at me to follow. She is desperately lonely. I am queasy as I hear her words. Will I go?

Is this all a crazy dream? Maybe things aren't so dramatically opposite. Or, maybe the answer lies somewhere in between, how I had imagined it.

Alone

Here I am alone again,
Without a friend.
Will this ever end?
I feel I must wait
Until fate
Plays itself out.
It's useless to shout.
Just dream of better times,
More sublime.

8 GOOD CABINS

Cabin By The Lake

Lowering behind the band of solid, impassive trees;
The sun is setting, making little sparks on the rippling water,
As it daily ought'er.
The trees and wind watch.
And so do I, to catch
The lovely endless cycle
Of waking and resting,
Lightening and darkening.
There must be a purpose
To all this beautiful fuss.
Something we are missing,
In all our scurrying.
Maybe it's peace and tranquility,
In all the passing iniquity.
Let's all pause daily
To sing gaily
With the little birds.
You might say those are good words;
"but I am too busy.
Always in a tizzy,
Can't find time
To be sublime".
Take the time
I promise you, it will be very fine!

Cabin In The Woods, Chapter 2

Silently, sitting on my comfortable cushion, gazing through the big picture window, I watch as the sun is sinking behind the darkening , shadowy band of trees in the distance. The golden orb is making little silvery glints on the rippling water. There is a gentle breeze blowing. The trees and I listen as the wind whispers in my ear about the endless cycles of waking and sleeping, dawning and darkening. It speaks to me softly: "Enjoy the peace and tranquility, in the midst of constant change and ups and downs".
There is something sweet and sacred in the sound of these words. My soul delights. The big bullfrog chorus croaks in agreement.

Then the curtain of darkness surrounds me. The silvery face of the moon rises in the quiet blackness, signaling a time to rest and dream; to dream sweet dreams of a brilliant new dawn.

9 A BAD CABIN

Cabin in Maine

On arrival, I was greeted by knee high grass,
Rickety floors; alas!
There was only one secure door.
This place, they need to restore.
Oh, there's more.
Water angrily spit out
Of all the downspouts,
Broken dishes, dirty pots.
It just does not stop.
Cramped space for the bed,
Cobwebs overhead,
Banged up doors.
Your rating will be poor.
Furnished with old, used stuff;
I almost left in a huff
When I could smell gas.
I stayed only to trip on the loose corner of the rug.
That made me say "Ugh!"
Get me out of the cobwebs, potholes, chipped paint
And bumpy road beds. I have more complaints:
The windows that let in the biting bugs.
This rundown place with the dirty mugs.
I can't blame the folks,
Who own this joke.
They are just trying to make a living.
The lake is well worth something.
But I will not come back
To this old shack.

10 EXTRATERRESTRIALS

Paradise Lost

I am an alien from another galaxy. Forty years ago, I visited earth. It was beautiful. I was describing Florida to my female companion. She got excited. So, we decided to hop into our space jalopy to see it. We arrived in a flash. We hid the saucer in a thicket for a fast get away. We resemble earthlings; so there would be no problem walking around. The landscape has changed drastically. It is now paved over. What happened?

My companion was hungry. We spied a food store not too far away. Crossing the six lane street at a run, as the impatient drivers rushed past the slow down sign. A bicycle was behind us and had a near miss with a car. Walkers need to beware of crossing these speed zones. Crossing the parking lot, we nearly were rammed by a car. He was very angry with us. He made some strange gesture with a finger. Oops, a biker is headed straight for us.

Sitting on the bench to calm ourselves down; we observed: tempers rise in tight parking lots, with drivers backing out into each other. Walking to your car is a game of survival with near misses No wonder a lot of people have unhappiness written all over their faces. Many own dogs with bared teeth, warning you to stay away or pay the price. Sometimes the owner lets the rope spool out; so that the dog can easily reach his intended prey.

There is much meanness, racism and gossiping.

My companion goes inside for a snack. I grab a newspaper to inform myself of local happenings. They have had an election. The new leader says he is going to shake up the U.S. (so that it can fall flat on its face).

That last part was an editorial comment.

I whisper to my companion but want to shout it out: "Stop, stop, stop all this madness! Aren't you all one human race, entitled to some happiness. Many people act like motherless children. I pray they all wake up and smell the roses."

We are leaving as fast as we can and never coming back.

ABOUT THE AUTHOR

Dolores Rollins was born in Biddeford, Maine in 1942. She has a BA in art education with a major in Fine Art. In a twist of fate, her life took a different turn after graduation; she taught Spanish and French at the High School level.

The book Silly Rhymes and the Sublime grew out of writing music with her husband of 48 years. That led to joining a writer's group, after his death.

This collection of lively short stories is a revealing insight into her daily experiences;. written with warmth, humor and spirituality.

www.ingramcontent.com/pod-product-compliance
Lightning Source LLC
Chambersburg PA
CBHW060619030426
42337CB00018B/3120